C000001487

ELECTROSTAR EMUs

Andrew Cole

AMBERLEY

First published 2020

Amberley Publishing
The Hill, Stroud
Gloucestershire, GL5 4EP

www.amberley-books.com

Copyright © Andrew Cole, 2020

The right of Andrew Cole to be identified as
the Author of this work has been asserted in
accordance with the Copyrights, Designs and
Patents Act 1988.

ISBN 978 1 4456 8217 4 (print)
ISBN 978 1 4456 8218 1 (ebook)

All rights reserved. No part of this book may be
reprinted or reproduced or utilised in any form
or by any electronic, mechanical or other means,
now known or hereafter invented, including
photocopying and recording, or in any information
storage or retrieval system, without the permission
in writing from the Publishers.

British Library Cataloguing in Publication Data.
A catalogue record for this book is available from
the British Library.

Typesetting by Aura Technology and Software
Services, India. Printed in the UK.

Introduction

The name Electrostar is used to encompass a family of Electric Multiple Units that were produced by Adtranz, later Bombardier, at their Derby works over an eighteen-year period. The Electrostar units were to become one of the main new build of EMUs following privatisation, and there are now a staggering 655 sets operating in the UK, almost exclusively in the south-east on the former Southern Region third-rail network. They can be found operating from three-car units through to five-car units.

There are seven different classes that come under the Electrostar umbrella, starting with the Class 357 units that are operated out of London Fenchurch Street on the London, Tilbury & Southend Railway. The Class 357 units resemble the Class 170 Turbostar diesel units, sharing the same cab design, the rest of the different classes having their own design.

The next class to emerge from Derby was the Class 375 units, built for use on the Southeastern lines out of Charing Cross and Canon Street into East Kent and Sussex. Built in five different batches, all are four-car units except for the ten three-car Class 375/3 units.

Then followed the Class 377 units built for Southern out of London Victoria and London Bridge, covering Sussex, Surrey, Kent and the south coast. There are seven different subclasses in the Class 377 number series, and they are the most numerous of the Electrostar units, totaling 239 units. They range from three-car sets through to five-car sets, and were built over a period of ten years. The Class 377/2 and Class 377/7 units are dual voltage and are able to operate both on the former Southern third-rail, as well as AC overhead, operating as far north as Milton Keynes Central.

The Class 376 units then followed, there being thirty-six commuter units for use by Southeastern out of Charing Cross and Canon Street on the lines to Dartford and Hayes. They were built without gangway connections between units and are five-car sets.

London Overground ordered a total of fifty-seven Class 378 units to replace to former Silverlink Class 313 units on Watford Junction DC lines, and also on the North London line. They were also introduced on the East London line, and now operate through to Clapham Junction. The first batch were introduced as three-car sets, and all have now had extra Motor Standard cars added, increasing them to five-car sets.

The thirty Class 379 units were introduced onto Stansted Express workings out of Liverpool Street, and are also used on Anglia services including through to Cambridge. The Class 379 units are due to be replaced by new Stadler-built Class 720 and 745 units in 2019.

The final class of Electrostar units are the Class 387 units. Twenty-nine units were built for Thameslink services from Brighton to Bedford but, following the introduction of Siemens-built Class 700 units, the Class 387 units transferred to Great Northern for use out of King's Cross on the Cambridge and King's Lynn routes. The second batch of units were ordered for Gatwick Express and there are twenty-seven units operating London Victoria to Brighton via Gatwick Airport, in their distinctive red livery. C2C took a further six Class 387/3 units on for use out of Fenchurch Street to compliment their existing fleet of Class 357 units.

The final members of the Electrostar fleet are forty-five units operated by Great Western Railway out of London Paddington on Reading, Didcot and Newbury services. They are also due to take over Heathrow Express services.

There is no doubting the success of the Electrostar family of units, in both helping to eradicate slam-door units on the Southern region, but also increasing passenger numbers and helping ease overcrowding on the intensive routes they serve. Their success also prompted an order for twenty-four units for use with Gautrain in South Africa for use around Johannesburg.

I hope you look forward to looking through this book, which captures these numerous units during their everyday use across the network.

Class 357

357001, 18 March 2017

357001 is seen making a station call at Barking. This was the very first Electrostar unit built by Adtranz at Derby. It was built in 1999, and was amongst the first electric EMUs delivered after privatisation. A further 654 units would follow it off the production line. It also carries the name *Barry Flaxman* on the other side of the cab.

357002 and 357046, 14 August 2017

357002 and 357046 stand side by side at Barking. Both are from the first batch of Class 357 units built. 357046 was one of two extra units built by Adtranz as compensation for the late delivery of the units. 357002 carries the name *Arthur Lewis Stride 1841–1922*.

357015, 14 August 2017

357015 is seen arriving at Barking with a C2C service to Shoeburyness. This class of unit have always been associated with the London, Tilbury and Southend route, and helped to eliminate the Class 302, Class 310 and Class 312 units from the route.

357020, 25 August 2018

357020 passes through Bethnal Green, while heading towards Barking. There are a few departures for the class from London Liverpool Street, especially on a weekend, although their main London terminus station is Fenchurch Street.

357021, 29 June 2015

357021 arrives at Barking with a service to Grays. At this time, the franchise was operated by National Express, and the unit is seen complete with National Express logos. It would later pass to Trenitalia.

357023, 25 August 2018

357023 stands in the dark confines of London Liverpool Street. This station is the main terminus for Anglia and London Overground services, but there are the occasional C2C services that operate out of and terminate there.

357025, 12 November 2016

357025 passes through a very dark and overcast Shadwell station, just outside Fenchurch Street, with a National Express working through to Shoeburyness. The line here runs parallel with the Docklands Light Railway.

357029, 29 June 2015

357029 is seen paused at Barking. When new, these units carried a very similar livery as to the one shown, but the doors were a dark green colour, and the green was also applied to the lower body panels. There then followed an all-over blue livery, before the class reverted to plain white. This unit carries the name *Thomas Whitelegg 1840–1922*.

357032, 25 March 2016

357032 departs from Upminster with a National Express C2C working. The C2C is thought to stand for Capital 2 Coast, but there is no specific reasoning behind the brand name.

357038, 14 August 2017

357038 departs from West Ham with a working towards Fenchurch Street. This is a very busy interchange point in East London, with three underground lines passing through, as well as the Docklands Light Railway.

357208, 7 September 2004

357208 arrives at Barking carrying the blue livery applied to the fleet not long after introduction. This livery was applied using vinyl, and was to last until around 2009 when they were removed. 357208 has since been named *Dave Davis*.

357216, 7 September 2004

357216 departs from Barking, heading towards Fenchurch Street. The Class 357 units use exactly the same design as their diesel Class 170 counterparts, with each car being a bit shorter. The similarity is easily seen with the Class 170 units belonging to the Turbostar family.

357227, 19 March 2013

357227 is seen making a station call at Barking while heading towards Fenchurch Street. During the time when National Express operated the franchise, a large number of the Class 357 fleet gained Union flag vinyls on the pantograph (PTSOL) car.

357313, 25 March 2016

357313 departs from Upminster. This unit appropriately enough carries the name *Upminster I. E. C. C.* and is one of seventeen members of the Class 357/2 fleet that have been renumbered.

357325, 12 November 2016

357325 is seen having passed through Shadwell, carrying National Express logos and the Union flag on the pantograph car. The Class 357/3 units have been reconfigured internally, having seats removed to create extra passenger space, they also carry pink 'Metro' stickers by the saloon doors.

Class 375

375301, 1 August 2013

375301 is seen at Ashford International with a Southeastern working towards London Charing Cross. There are just ten of the Class 375/3 units in service, and they differ from the main batches in that they only consist of three cars rather than the usual four.

375302, 8 August 2013

375302 is seen approaching London Bridge with a service towards the capital. The unit is seen carrying the livery in which all of the Class 375 units were delivered, plain white but with yellow saloon doors, although some later gained grey lower bodyside panels.

375307, 17 March 2017

375307 is seen making a call at Elephant & Castle station. The unit is seen carrying the newly applied blue livery that the whole class now carries. The repainting was carried out at Derby when the class were refurbished from 2015 onwards.

375308, 12 June 2012

375308 is seen having arrived at Ashford International. A small number of the class received light blue doors, replacing the standard yellow doors, as can be seen on 375308.

375601, 9 June 2015

375601 is seen arriving at Ashford International. This was the first Class 375 unit built by Adtranz at Derby, and entered service in 2001. There are currently 112 Class 375 units in service with Southeastern spread over five different subclasses.

375602, 29 March 2016

375602 is seen arriving at Tonbridge, having just emerged from the nearby carriage sidings. At this time, the refurbishment of the class was well underway, and there weren't too many Class 375/6 units left in the original livery.

375603, 2 August 2017

375603 passes through New Cross, just outside of London Bridge, as part of an eight-car Southeastern working. Both units carry the refurbished blue livery.

375605, 29 March 2016

375605 arrives at Tonbridge having passed through the refurbishment programme. Of note is the front fly door, which hasn't been locked properly and has sprung back open, creating a draughty cab for the driver.

375606, 29 March 2016

375606 is seen making a call at Tonbridge in the spring sunshine. The blue livery applied to these units was in stark contrast to the white livery they were all delivered carrying.

375608, 8 August 2013

375608 is seen at London Bridge while heading for Charing Cross. In this view, the name *Bromley Travelwise*, which was carried by this unit at the time, can just be made out on the second carriage. Since refurbishment, the name has been removed.

375609, 9 June 2015

375609 is seen arriving at Ashford International. The unit is seen carrying the revised Southeastern livery, similar to that carried by the Class 465 Networker units, of grey lower body sides and blue passenger doors.

375610, 8 August 2013

375610 is seen at London Bridge. This unit was different to the rest of the fleet at the time, as it carried blue saloon doors rather than the usual yellow, and it also carried the name *Royal Tunbridge Wells*, which can be seen on the second carriage.

375612, 2 August 2017

375612 is seen arriving at Lewisham, across the myriad of diamond crossovers at this station. The unit carries refurbished Southeastern blue livery.

375614, 29 March 2016

375614 departs from Tonbridge, heading for London Charing Cross. The busy GBRf freight yard can just be glimpsed in the background.

375615, 4 October 2016

375615 is seen at Ashford International, having arrived from London. The overhead lines to the left are for the high-speed line for the Eurostar units from London St Pancras International to the Channel Tunnel.

375623, 1 August 2013

375623 departs from the very picturesque Dover Priory station towards Ramsgate. Of note is the signal box still in situ on the opposite platform. At the time, 375623 carried the name *Hospice in the Weald*.

375626, 29 March 2016

375626 is seen at Tonbridge carrying Southeastern blue livery. The yellow area on the second carriage denotes first class, and the Claret area on the third vehicle denotes the wheelchair space. The Class 375/6 units carry pantographs and are the only members of the Class 375 units to do so.

375626, 14 August 2016

375626 departs from Robertsbridge, past one of the many delightful signal boxes still to be seen on the Southern region. The unit is working towards Hastings.

375701, 29 March 2016

375701 is seen at Tonbridge prior to refurbishment. At the time, 375701 carried the name *Kent Air Ambulance Explorer.*

375703, 29 March 2016

375703 stands at Ashford International. This view shows the standard layout of the whole fleet at the time, the only exceptions being later builds had modified headlight clusters.

375705, 29 March 2016

375705 is seen at Ashford International. The platforms to the right are for the international services and are out of bounds for everyday use and passengers. 375705 carries the later Southeastern livery, only carried by a small handful of Class 375 units.

375715, 2 August 2017

375715 passes through New Cross on its way to London Charing Cross. It is seen coupled to an unrefurbished example, and the difference in the liveries is quite apparent. 375715 was the last of the Class 375/7 subclass.

375802, 13 May 2008

375802 is seen at London Bridge alongside Class 376 376036. This view shows the two different styles of front end between the two different classes. This view has completely changed now, following the rebuilding of the station.

375804, 14 June 2017

375804 arrives at Tonbridge as part of a twelve-car Southeastern working. 375804 carries refurbished blue livery, whereas the unit coupled has yet to visit Derby for refurbishment. Tonbridge station is the junction from the South Eastern Main Line to Dover from the line to Hastings.

375806, 14 August 2016

375806 passes through Robertsbridge on its way to London. This station also has the delightful Rother Valley Railway adjacent, and is situated to the right behind the trees.

375809, 1 August 2013

375809 passes underneath the magnificent signal box at Canterbury West. This line branches off at Ashford International and heads towards Ramsgate.

375813, 2 March 2019

375813 is seen making a call at the newly rebuilt London Bridge station. The station was rebuilt to better accommodate the through Thameslink workings, operated by Class 700 units, from Brighton to Bedford.

375815, 12 November 2016

375815 passes by New Cross station as part of an eight-car unrefurbished Southeastern working. New Cross is also served by London Overground, with their services to Dalston Junction.

375819, 9 September 2017

375819 is seen being hauled through Clapham Junction by Class 37 37800, after being refurbished at Bombardier Derby. The unit is being returned to Ramsgate depot prior to re-entering service. Class 375s aren't normally seen at Clapham Junction.

375820, 14 August 2016

375820 is seen arriving at London Bridge in unrefurbished condition. This was taken during the time when London Bridge was being rebuilt and, since this shot was taken, the work has been completed, and includes more overhead shelter.

375825, 1 August 2013

375825 is seen arriving at Canterbury West with a Southeastern working towards London Charing Cross. At the time the signal box was still very much in use.

375908, 21 July 2016

375908 arrives at London Bridge with a Southeastern working towards Charing Cross. The Class 375 fleet took six years to build, from 1999 to 2005, and they helped eliminate the old slam door Southern stock from services in Kent.

375911, 2 August 2017

375911 passes through New Cross with a Southeastern working towards Hastings. This is a very busy station, located just outside London Bridge, with services increasing throughout the peak hours.

375913, 1 August 2013

375913 is seen stabled at Dover Priory ready for the afternoon peak services. This view shows the grey edging applied to the lower body panels on some of the class members; not all received them before being refurbished.

375918, 1 August 2013

375918 is seen departing from Dover Priory while heading towards London Charing Cross. Class 395 395003 stands alongside, waiting to depart for London St Pancras International, the trains taking the same line to Ashford before going their own separate ways.

375921, 29 March 2016

375921 is seen arriving at Headcorn with a Southeastern working towards Ashford International. This is on the line between Ashford and Tonbridge.

Class 376

376001, 9 September 2017

376001 is seen departing from New Cross on a sunny autumn day while heading for Charing Cross. There are thirty-six Class 376 units in service with Southeastern, and they are used on local services, being fitted with high-density seating.

376002, 12 November 2016

376002 works non-stop through New Cross. The unit carries the livery all members of the class were delivered in, and they all still carry this livery today.

376005, 8 August 2013

376005 is seen making a station call at London Bridge. The Class 376 units are normally confined to Dartford and Hayes workings, as they are high-volume routes. The units are five carriages in length and utilise the maximum loading gauge possible.

376009, 21 July 2016

376009 arrives at London Bridge during the station's refurbishment. The units date from 2004, and helped to eliminate the former Southern region slam-door stock from Kent.

376010, 2 August 2017

376010 is seen on the approach to Lewisham station coming over the flyover and is about to pass over the mass of diamond crossovers. An unusual feature of the Class 376 units is the lack of gangway connection on the front of the unit, quite unusual for modern units on the former Southern region.

376013, 21 July 2016

376013 stands at London Bridge with a Southeastern working into the capital. Another unusual feature on these units is the windscreen wiper fitted to the centre screen, as there can't really be much use for it.

376018, 12 November 2016

376018 is seen passing under the Lewisham Arms pub as it passes through New Cross on its way into the capital. The whole class have been allocated to Slade Green depot for their entire careers.

376021, 9 September 2017

376021 is seen making a station call at New Cross. This view shows off the units five-car formation, an unusual sight on the former Southern region, with most units being four-car length.

376025, 8 August 2013

376025 is seen arriving at London Bridge with another working into the capital. This view was taken before the station was rebuilt yet, during the rebuild, services kept running.

376036, 21 July 2016

376036 is seen arriving at London Bridge with a Southeastern working through to Hayes. These units are due for refurbishment in the near future, so it will be interesting to see if they emerge in blue to match the Class 375 units.

Class 377

377109, 14 June 2017

377109 works non-stop through Gatwick Airport. The unit carries Southern livery, with Southern operating the vast majority of the Class 377 units. There are a total of 239 Class 377s in use, in various configurations and train lengths.

377112, 17 March 2017

377112 is seen slowing for the station call at Clapham Junction while heading towards London Victoria. The Class 377/1 units date from 2002, and there are sixty-four of this subclass in service.

377122, 9 June 2015

377122 is seen as it arrives at Brighton with a terminating service from London Victoria. The Class 377 units run in various formations down to Brighton, from four-car trains up to twelve-car formations.

377125, 13 May 2008

377125 is seen arriving at London Bridge with a terminating service. This side of London Bridge is used by Southern, whereas the lines to the left are used by Southeastern and Thameslink.

377128 and 387128, 9 June 2015

377128 and 387128 are seen side by side at Brighton. This view shows the Southern livery applied to 377128 and the Thameslink livery applied to 387128. Despite being built ten years apart, this view also shows how little the design has changed over the years, the only difference being the more intense headlights on 387128.

377133, 23 September 2016

377133 is seen departing from Gatwick Airport in the autumn sunshine with a Southern working through to London Victoria. Over on the far platform a Class 387/2 can be seen carrying Gatwick Express red livery.

377134 and 377321, 29 March 2016

377134 and 377321 are seen stabled side by side at Tonbridge, adjacent to the freight yard. The units have been used on morning peak services and are stabled ready for the afternoon peak to start.

377143, 8 August 2013

377143 is seen stabled in-between duties at East Grinstead. This is the terminating station on this line, and the line to the right is the preserved Bluebell Line. The line the Class 377 is stabled on is actually the connection between the preserved line and the Network Rail lines.

377206, 3 February 2015

377206 is seen having just departed from Wembley Central while working to Milton Keynes Central. The Class 377/2 units are fitted with pantographs and are dual voltage to enable them to work to Milton Keynes. The leading unit with 377206 is 377204.

377208, 9 June 2015

377208 is seen passing through Elephant & Castle. Not a usual haunt for Class 377/2s, this particular unit was on hire from Southern to Thameslink as cover and, as can be seen, carries Thameslink logos over the Southern ones.

377210, 20 January 2009

377210 is seen waiting to depart from Watford Junction for South Croydon. The first few services of the day started at Watford instead of working up to Milton Keynes. The changeover from AC traction to DC traction usually occurs after the train has gone over the Great Western Main Line near North Pole depot.

377210, 9 June 2015

377210 is seen arriving at Elephant & Castle with a Thameslink working to Bedford. With the Class 377/2 units being dual voltage, they were the perfect choice for hiring to Thameslink from Southern.

377210, 25 February 2017

377210 is seen making a station call at St Pancras International. This was still on hire to Thameslink at the time, but by now the Thameslink logos had been removed. Thameslink now only use Siemens-built Class 700 units.

377211, 9 June 2015

377211 is seen departing from Brighton, heading for Bedford. This unit at the time was operated by Southern, but it was on hire to Thameslink, whose logos it carries, but it had also been hired by First Capital Connect, whose livery it carries.

377214, 28 April 2014

377214 is seen arriving at Milton Keynes Central with a terminating Southern working. It would later head back south towards South Croydon at 08.13. Prior to the Class 377s introduction on these services, a Class 319 was used to work up as far as Rugby before the service was curtailed at Milton Keynes.

377305, 17 March 2017

377305 is seen passing through Tulse Hill in London with a Southern working. The Class 377/3 subclass are only formed of three carriages and can sometimes operate as four units coupled together to make twelve-car formations.

377307, 2 August 2017

377307 is seen arriving at a wet Oxted. The Class 377/3 units were originally delivered as Class 375/3 units, numbered 311–338, but they had their couplings changed from Tightlock to Dellner, thus meaning they were renumbered to Class 377/3s.

377322, 8 August 2013

377322 is seen stabled at East Grinstead, waiting for the afternoon peak services to start. During the day, the platform that the unit is occupying isn't used for passenger services, it being used as a stabling platform.

377323, 26 October 2017

377323 is seen also stabled at East Grinstead waiting for the afternoon peak services. All of the Southern-operated Class 377 units still carry the livery they were delivered in, with the Class 377/3 dating from 2001. Even the units in Thameslink vinyl livery have reverted to Southern livery.

377342, 17 March 2017

377342 is seen as part of an eleven-car working at Clapham Junction. This unit was originally delivered as 377442 but, following a fire in one of its centre cars, it was put back into service as a three-car Class 377/3 and renumbered to 377342.

377402, 8 September 2014

377402 is seen arriving at Gatwick Airport from the south. The unit is running as an eight-car formation, coupled to a similar unit. All of the Class 377 subclasses are able to work in multiple with each other.

377409, 8 August 2013

377409 is seen as it departs from London Bridge with a Southern working. Alongside can be seen Class 319 319421 arriving with a Thameslink service. These were to be replaced by Siemens-built Class 700 units.

377412 and 377444, 9 June 2015

377412 and 377444 are seen stabled side by side at Brighton Lovers Walk depot. This is where a large number of the Southern Class 377s are based, although there are some members of the class allocated to Selhurst. The lines to the left are the Coastway lines towards Portsmouth.

377419, 9 June 2015

377419 is seen arriving into Brighton from the Coastway route. There are seventy-four Class 377/4 units in service, dating from 2004, although one has been converted to a Class 377/3 following a fire.

377430, 9 June 2015

377430 is seen having just arrived at Brighton station with a terminating Southern service. The Thameslink-liveried Class 387 alongside has already been displaced from Thameslink workings by the Class 700 units, and they can now be found on Great Northern services out of London King's Cross.

377442, 19 September 2016

377442 is seen departing from Gatwick Airport. A couple of months after this shot was taken, there would be an internal fire in one of the centre carriages, which resulted in the unit being returned to service as a three-car unit, and has been renumbered 377342.

377444, 377441 and 377161, 4 July 2013

377444, 377441 and 377161 are all seen at Clapham Junction. This view is evidence as to why Clapham Junction is one of the busiest stations on the entire network, with a vigorous operation that gets more intense during peak hours.

377455 and 456023, 8 August 2013

377455 and 456023 are seen side by side at London Bridge. This is another very busy location in the capital, with services only becoming more intense during the peak. In this view five different trains can be seen coming and going.

377461, 14 October 2017

377461 is seen arriving at Haywards Heath with a Southern working to London Victoria. The Class 377 units helped to eradicate the former Southern region slam-door stock from the south-east.

377466 and 442401, 20 April 2015

377466 and 442401 are seen side by side at Clapham Junction. Since this view, the Class 442 units have been displaced from Gatwick Express duties by Electrostar Class 387/2 units and, after time in storage, they are beginning to return to service.

377501, 4 July 2013

377501 is seen at Brighton having just arrived from Bedford. The unit carries First Capital Connect livery. The Class 377/5 units were the only subclass not operated by Southern, but they had Southern spec interiors.

377503, 17 March 2017

377503 is seen passing through Clapham Junction with an empty stock move. The unit is seen carrying Southeastern livery and, after Thameslink had finished using them, the twenty-three units passed to Southeastern to help increase capacity on their lines.

377505, 9 June 2015

377505 is seen at Brighton. By this time, First Capital Connect had lost the running of the Thameslink franchise and the units now came under the franchise operated by Govia. The unit is seen still carrying First Capital Connect livery, but with Thameslink logos.

377513, 17 March 2017

377513 is seen arriving at Elephant & Castle with a Thameslink working through to Bedford. By this time, the former First 'dynamic block' livery had been changed to plain blue, the units just retaining their Thameslink logos. They would soon be displaced by Class 700 units from Siemens.

377514, 14 June 2017

377514 is seen approaching Redhill with a Thameslink working to Three Bridges. With their workings taking them as far north as Bedford, the Class 377/5 units were also dual voltage, similar to the Class 377/2 units, with the changeover point being Farringdon from AC to DC traction.

377516, 17 March 2017

377516 snakes round into Tulse Hill station, working together with classmate 377510. By this time, the Class 377/5 units had already started being transferred to Southeastern and were soon to all be transferred.

377517, 3 November 2017

377517 is seen having arrived at Ashford International on a cold autumn evening. Despite the unit carrying Thameslink logos, it was in fact operated by Southeastern, having recently transferred over to help with capacity on the lines in Kent.

377518, 17 March 2017

377518 is seen departing from Elephant & Castle with a Thameslink working to Bedford. This view shows the first class end of the train, as denoted by the large yellow stripe, but it also has first class lettering on the side.

377521, 19 June 2017

377521 is seen in the dark confines of St Pancras International with a Thameslink working to Elephant & Castle. The frequency of units passing through this part of St Pancras is phenomenal, especially during the peak hours.

377523, 9 June 2015

377523 is seen arriving at Elephant & Castle, running as just a single four-car working. At the time, this station was incredibly busy due to all Thameslink services passing through. Now the chord has opened between London Blackfriars and London Bridge, the Brighton services and some of the Sutton services go that way instead.

377607, 9 September 2017

377607 is seen departing from Norwood Junction while heading towards London Victoria. There are twenty-six Class 377/6 units in service, and they are formed as five-car units. They are most often seen working in pairs, creating ten-car trains, and are mainly used on suburban routes in the capital.

377611, 17 March 2017

377611 is seen making a station call at Clapham Junction while heading towards London Victoria. One noticeable difference between the Class 377/6 units and the earlier subclasses are the thicker window rubbers used, making them easily identifiable.

377612, 14 October 2017

377612 passes through Three Bridges non-stop with a ten-car Southern working. The station was busy on this day due to there being an open day at the nearby Siemens depot where they were showing off their new fleet of Class 700 units.

377616, 17 March 2017

377616 is seen arriving at Clapham Junction with a Southern working from London Victoria. Clapham Junction is a great place to see the Southern Class 377 units working, as the units pass through on a very regular basis, working in and out of London Victoria.

377621, 12 November 2013

377621 is seen on Bescot depot in the West Midlands. With the units being built at Derby, they needed to be hauled to the Southern region to take up service. Having been stabled in the yard at Bescot, 377621 suffered a graffiti attack, which resulted in it being shunted into the depot for it to be removed. It spent around a week on the depot. Of note is the emergency coupling fitted on the front.

377622, 14 October 2017

377622 passes through Three Bridges while on its way to London Victoria. Note the additional extra light on the front of the unit, a feature that is creeping in on all modern unit deliveries in the UK.

377701 and 377608, 17 March 2017

377701 and 377608 are seen side by side at Clapham Junction. The eight Class 377/7 units are also dual voltage units, and they are intended for use on the West Coast Main Line to Milton Keynes, replacing the Class 377/2 units. They are run in five-car formations, thus increasing the capacity, but can also be seen paired with Class 377/6 units on suburban workings.

377704, 3 February 2015

377704 is seen departing from Hemel Hempstead while working from Milton Keynes Central down to South Croydon. The units take the West Coast Main Line to Willesden Junction, before branching off towards Kensington Olympia, and then coming up through Clapham Junction.

377705, 20 April 2015

377705 departs from Clapham Junction, heading for South Croydon. The Class 377/7s were the last of the type ordered by Southern, and were built in 2014, thirteen years after the first Class 377 units were built.

377707, 26 June 2014

377707 is seen stabled at Rugby. Before the Class 377/7s were introduced, they were tested on the West Coast Main Line to accumulate fault-free mileage turns, a feature that most of the new units built by Bombardier have to complete, with most new units being tested in this way.

Class 378

378135, 18 March 2017

378135 is seen arriving at Hoxton, just south of Dalston Junction. The Class 378 units are operated by London Overground and, like the Class 376 units, they don't have gangway doors on the front of the units. However, an emergency evacuation door is fitted in the centre of the cab front.

378137, 17 March 2017

378137 is seen departing from Clapham Junction, carrying the original London Overground livery applied to the whole class from new. This view shows how the saloon doors don't sit flush with the bodyside, but are recessed slightly inwards, the bodywork maximizing the loading gauge.

378138, 22 March 2013

378138 is seen arriving at Surrey Quays. This is the main junction on the line where services for New Cross split off from the other lines to Crystal Palace, West Croydon and Clapham Junction.

378139, 12 November 2016

378139 is seen arriving at Shadwell while working towards Highbury & Islington. The Class 378/1 units are only equipped with third rail operation, and so can only be used on the former South London line and East London lines. They helped to replace London Transport underground stock from the line.

378140 and 378150, 13 June 2013

378140 and 378150 are seen approaching and departing from Canonbury. A third unit can be seen in the distance, which is at Highbury & Islington, the terminus station for this part of the route, it being the next departure behind 378140.

378141, 20 April 2015

378141 is seen arriving at Clapham Junction running as a five-car train. The unit is arriving from Highbury & Islington. Clapham Junction is a changeover point where these lines meet the lines that go up through Willesden Junction and around towards Stratford.

378141, 12 November 2016

378141 is seen making a station call at Dalston Junction. The unit displays a headboard stating the fact that the unit has been strengthened to five cars. The Class 378/1 fleet was built as four-car units, with them all receiving a new centre car in 2015/16.

378143, 22 March 2013

378143 is seen departing from Surrey Quays while heading for New Cross. Although the East London line is only fitted for third rail operation, dual voltage Class 378/2 units can also appear on the route.

378144, 18 March 2017

378144 is seen departing from Whitechapel on the East London line. By this time, most of the units had lost their five-car adverts from the front of the unit. Whitechapel is a busy interchange station, with the District, Hammersmith and City London Underground lines passing through as well.

378145, 18 March 2017

378145 is seen rounding the curve into Hoxton station. The unit is heading for Highbury & Islington. There are twenty Class 378/1 units in use, and they have largely remained as delivered with just the introduction of a fifth carriage, although a start has been made on repainting them into the new London Overground livery.

378148, 18 March 2017

378148 is seen arriving at Hoxton. This view shows how the unit is running as a five-car train and, due to the platform lengths, the London Overground fleet never run in pairs, always just a single unit.

378150, 2 March 2019

378150 is seen arriving at Clapham Junction. The unit is seen carrying the new version of the London Overground livery, which is similar to that which is carried by the new Class 710 units that are being delivered. Note that the position of the running number has been moved from the front of the unit to on the front corner, just by the headlight cluster.

378153, 3 February 2015

The new centre carriage for unit 378153 is seen at Wembley whilst being delivered from Bombardier, at Derby, down to the depot at New Cross. Some of the centre cars travelled singularly, or multiple car moves occurred. The car is seen sandwiched between two translator vans, which are fitted with couplings to allow the car to be moved.

378202, 4 October 2016

378202 is seen at Watford Junction, having arrived from London Euston. When the Class 378/2 units were introduced on this line, they only ran as three-car units, and were numbered in the Class 378/0 series, but they soon gained a fourth car and were renumbered into the Class 378/2 series. They are due to be replaced on this route by new Class 710 units.

378204, 19 March 2013

378204 is seen slowing for the station call at Kensington Olympia. Services on this line either start at Clapham Junction or Richmond and travel round to Stratford, via Willesden Junction and Gospel Oak. At this time, 378204 was still running as a four-car unit.

378205, 11 August 2016

378205 is seen on the buffer stops at Watford Junction. The Class 378 units are internally fitted with longitudinal seating, similar to London Transport underground trains. This was done to increase capacity during busy periods, and indeed the services out of Clapham Junction are heavily used throughout the day.

378207, 4 October 2016

378207 is seen at London Euston prior to departing for Watford Junction. It is seen alongside what were then London Midland Class 350 units, but these have now passed to West Midlands Trains and run under the London Northwestern Railway banner.

378211, 4 July 2013

378211 is seen arriving at Clapham Junction. The unit is seen carrying an overall advert for Lycamobile and was one of two Class 378 units to do so, 378221 being the other. The advert was carried on all four cars at the time, and it has since been removed from both units.

378214, 13 June 2013

378214 stands in the summer sunshine at Clapham Junction. This will soon depart for Stratford, travelling via Kensington Olympia, Willesden Junction and Gospel Oak. It cant be underestimated just how important the London Overground routes are in linking other lines in the capital.

378215, 12 March 2015

378215 runs into Canonbury station. This is not far from the terminus at Stratford and is one of the stations where the London Overground lines meet, this being the Stratford to Clapham Junction and Richmond line, with the East London line to New Cross, Crystal Palace and Clapham Junction on the right of the island platform.

378217, 12 November 2016

378217 is seen departing from Dalston Junction, heading for Clapham Junction, and is seen carrying its five-car advert on the front. The unit is seen climbing the steep incline out of the station, and the next station, Haggerston, can be seen at the top of the incline.

378219, 3 February 2015

378219 is seen slowing for the station call at Carpenders Park. This is on the line to Watford Junction, and the units use their third rail DC equipment on this route. There were originally thirty-four Class 378/2 units, but a further three were ordered as a follow-on order.

378219, 12 March 2015

378219 is seen passing the depot at Willesden while heading for Watford Junction. The DC lines run underneath the West Coast lines just south of Wembley Central. Willesden Junction is another important interchange point on the London Overground network, where the Watford Junction lines intersect with the lines towards Kensington Olympia and Gospel Oak.

378221, 19 March 2013

378221 is seen arriving at Gospel Oak with a working to Stratford. As can be seen, the unit carries adverts for Lycamobile but they have since been removed. Gospel Oak is where the lines to Stratford meet the North London lines through to Barking.

378221, 16 June 2015

The centre car for unit 378221 is seen at Bescot, en route from Bombardier, at Derby, down to New Cross. There are also three more centre cars for units 378222, 224 and 225, which will allow the units to be increased to five-car trains. An unusual sight in the West Midlands.

378222, 19 March 2013

378222 is seen having departed from Willesden Junction, heading for Clapham Junction. The units run off the AC overhead wires on this route, so the Class 378/1 units cannot operate here.

378223 and 378212, 3 February 2015

378223 and 378212 are seen passing each other at South Kenton on the line to Watford Junction. At this time, the units were still operating as four-car units but would soon be increased up to five-car trains. Closer to London, the Class 378 units on this route share the same tracks as the London Transport Underground trains. The Class 378 units on this route are due to be replaced by Bombardier-built Class 710 Aventra units.

378224 and 378257, 12 March 2015

378224 and 378257 are seen arriving and departing from Gospel Oak. 378224 was originally delivered carrying the number 378024 but was renumbered when it received a fourth carriage. 378257 was the very last Class 378 delivered and formed part of the last three add-on units.

378226, 14 October 2017

378226 is seen as it approaches Bushey on the line to Watford Junction. This scene will soon be history when the Bombardier-built Class 710 units enter service.

378227, 2 August 2017

378227 is seen departing from Hackney Central whilst working towards Stratford. This station is where the Stratford lines meet the lines from Chingford, Cheshunt and Enfield Town from Liverpool Street, the two lines being joined by a long covered walkway.

378228, 12 November 2016

378228 arrives at Willesden Junction with its headlight piercing the gloom on a wet and miserable autumn day. The unit proudly displays its five-car advert on the emergency evacuation door.

378233, 12 November 2016

378233 is seen departing from Camden Road while on its way to Stratford. This unit carries the name *Ian Brown CBE*, who was the former Managing Director of London Rail at Transport for London.

378257, 12 March 2015

378257 arrives at Canonbury while working towards Stratford. The last three Class 378 units were delivered in 2011 and, being dual voltage, were numbered in the 378/2 series, giving a total of thirty-seven dual voltage units numbered 378201–378234 and 378255–378257, with the Class 378/1 units numbered 378135–378154.

Class 379

379001, 2 August 2017

379001 is seen climbing up the incline towards Bethnal Green, having just departed from Liverpool Street with a Greater Anglia working through to Stansted Airport. There are thirty Class 379 units in use, all with Greater Anglia. They are used on Stansted Express workings but can also be found on Cambridge services.

379003, 2 August 2017

379003 passes through Bethnal Green with a Greater Anglia Stansted Express working to Liverpool Street. Theses units were introduced in 2011 and, despite their youthful age, they are already due to be replaced by Stadler-built Class 745 units, with currently no new operator found for the units.

379008, 25 August 2018

379008 passes through Bethnal Green while heading for Cambridge. The Class 379 units carry Greater Anglia logos on the driving cars, and Stansted Express logos on the two centre cars. The introduction of these units helped to eliminate the Class 317 units from this route.

379011, 29 August 2018

379011 stands on the buffer stops at Liverpool Street before departing for Stansted Airport with a Stansted Express working. This unit carries the name *Ely Cathedral*. The plate can be seen fitted above the first saloon window on the side.

379019, 8 June 2016

379019 waits for departure time at Liverpool Street with a Stansted Express working through to the airport. Most of these services are formed of eight-car units, two coupled in multiple.

379023, 2 August 2017

379023 passes non-stop through Bethnal Green heading for Liverpool Street. This is an incredibly busy station, being the first stop outside Liverpool Street, with suburban and long distance trains to Norwich passing through.

Class 387

387101, 25 February 2017

387101 is seen at London King's Cross. The Class 387 units are the final units built in the Electrostar family, with 107 units in use by four different operators.

387102, 25 August 2018

387102 passes through Alexandra Palace with a Great Northern working through to King's Cross. The first twenty-nine Class 387/1 units were originally delivered to Thameslink to provide extra capacity and to help eliminate the Class 319 units, but they were replaced themselves by the Class 700 units, so they all transferred to Great Northern.

387103, 14 August 2017

387103 stands on the buffer stops at King's Cross with a Great Northern working. Following their introduction on these lines, a start was made in placing the Class 365 units, which had been on the route for over twenty years, into storage.

387104, 9 June 2015

387104 arrives at Brighton with a Thameslink working from Bedford. The Class 387/1 units for Thameslink were introduced in 2015 but would only stay on the route for a couple of years before heading to Great Northern.

387106, 9 June 2015

387106 is seen arriving at Elephant & Castle with a Thameslink working. Following the transfer to Great Northern, the only change made on the units were the logos on the side.

387108, 9 June 2015

387108 is seen waiting to depart from Brighton with a Thameslink working. Despite the Class 387/1 units departing from this route, Class 387/2 units still visit with Gatwick Express units working through to Brighton.

387111, 1 December 2014

387111 is seen passing through Rugeley Trent Valley in Staffordshire while on a mileage accumulation test run before entering service with Thameslink. All of the Class 387 units have done similar test runs on the West Coast Main Line, a practice that continues with the Bombardier-built Aventra units doing the same.

387112, 1 December 2014

387112 is seen approaching Rugeley Trent Valley while on a mileage accumulation test run on a dull and overcast winter's day. Of note is the light fitted to observe the pantograph, another modern feature on new built units.

387114, 25 August 2018

387114 is seen approaching Alexandra Palace as part of an eight-car Great Northern working to Peterborough. The Class 387 units have a maximum speed of 110 mph, although the Great Northern examples are limited to 100 mph.

387120, 25 February 2017

387120 is seen in the Main Line platforms at King's Cross. The unit is waiting to depart with a Great Northern stopping service to Letchworth, where the service terminated due to engineering work. The introduction of the Class 387s to Great Northern allowed the Class 317 unit alongside to be cascaded to Anglia.

387121, 19 September 2016

387121 makes a station call at Gatwick Airport while working a Thameslink service through to Brighton. The Class 387s displaced Class 319 units from Thameslink, most of which were cascaded north to work for Northern, although some are also being converted to Class 769 'Flex' units.

387122, 10 June 2017

387122 is seen at Peterborough having arrived with a terminating Great Northern working. The Class 387s helped eliminate some of the Class 365 units from Great Northern. Some went on hire to Scotrail as a short-term stopgap until the new Class 385 units entered service north of the border.

387124, 17 March 2017

387124 passes through Clapham Junction on the back of a Gatwick Express working to London Victoria. This was on temporary hire to Gatwick Express from Thameslink as cover while one of their Class 387/2 units returned to Derby for repairs. 387124 is seen devoid of branding and was hired as Govia operated both franchises at the time.

387130, 18 March 2017

387130 is seen on the buffer stops at London Paddington. This was the first of an order for forty-five Class 387/1 units made by Great Western Railway. Most of the services are operated as eight-car workings, with the electrification eventually extending into South Wales.

387131 and 360205, 27 January 2018

387131 and 360205 are seen side by side at Ealing Broadway. The Class 360 unit was built by Siemens, Germany, in 2004 and carries a unique Heathrow Express livery. The Class 387 was operating a Great Western Railway service to Reading.

387132, 29 July 2016

387132 is seen working north through Nuneaton while on a mileage accumulation run. These workings started at Wembley yard, and went as far north as Crewe. The unit carries Great Western Railway green livery, but has yet to receive its GWR logos.

387133, 29 July 2016

387133 works north through Nuneaton, along with classmate Class 387, 387132, while on a mileage accumulation run to Crewe. All of the Class 387s from all operators have done the same runs, bringing some very strangely liveried units to the West Coast Main Line.

387136, 27 January 2018

387136 departs from Ealing Broadway as the rear unit of an eight-car Great Western Railway working to London Paddington. The Class 387/1s are due to take over the Heathrow Express workings from the Class 332 units, which will be cascaded elsewhere.

387139, 18 March 2017

387139 is seen making a station call at Acton Main Line while working to Hayes & Harlington. This was when the Class 387s had just entered service with GWR. Of note is that the platforms have yet to be extended, resulting in the unit operating selective door opening, with the very rear carriage being locked out at this station.

387141, 2 June 2018

387141 is seen at Reading, having arrived with a terminating service from London Paddington. Following the introduction of the Class 387 units, a new depot and sidings were opened to the west of the station, replacing the old DMU depot, which was taken over as a stabling point for on-track plant vehicles.

387144, 2 February 2017

387144 is seen working southbound through Rugeley Trent Valley while on a mileage accumulation run. Of note is the fact that 387144 carries full GWR green livery, complete with logos. Earlier units ran in plain green.

387151, 27 January 2018

387151 is seen inside the very impressive train shed at London Paddington. Alongside a Class 43 power car can be seen, a sight soon to disappear from London Paddington following the introduction of Hitachi-built Class 800 units, with the remaining power cars being used in the West of England.

387155, 14 June 2017

387155 is seen running through Gatwick Airport on another mileage accumulation run. As the GWR Class 387/1 units are also fitted with third rail shoegear and running equipment, they also needed to have test runs on the third rail, the units working as far as Brighton.

387172, 29 January 2018

387172 is seen running into a gloomy Reading station with an empty coaching stock move. Note how the small light on the front pierces the gloom. The unit ran through the station and stabled on the new depot to the west of the station.

387201, 23 September 2016

387201 is seen arriving at Gatwick Airport while operating a Gatwick Express service to Brighton. This was the first Class 387/2 out of a total of twenty-seven units ordered by Gatwick Express. They helped to eliminate the Derby-built Class 442 units from these services. The Class 387/2 units were delivered before the final batch of Class 387/1 units for GWR.

387202, 25 March 2016

387202 is seen passing through Elephant & Castle. Before the class was introduced onto Gatwick Express services, a handful of units were hired to fellow Govia-operated franchise Thameslink to increase capacity. The units operated in plain red livery, without branding.

387203, 25 March 2016

387203 is seen approaching Elephant & Castle while on hire to Thameslink. The red livery, carried by the Class 387/2 units, was a radical departure at the time as most new units were delivered carrying white livery, with just local variations.

387205 and 377426, 14 June 2017

387205 and 377426 are seen side by side at Gatwick Airport. Despite the fact that the two units were built over ten years apart, the design, as can be seen, is exactly the same, the only difference being the small light carried on the front cowling on 387205.

387205, 14 June 2017

387205 is seen at Brighton, having just arrived from London Victoria. This view shows the large 'GX' logo on the side, along with the Gatwick Express branding and white stripe, which compliments the red livery perfectly.

387206, 9 September 2017

387206 is seen approaching Clapham Junction as part of an eight-car Gatwick Express working to Gatwick Airport. These units are fitted for driver-only operation, with the large pods on the side of the carriages being the cameras that relay the images to the driver.

387207 and 700119, 10 May 2018

387207 and 700119 are seen side by side at Gatwick Airport. This view shows the startling front-end differences between the two modern designs of EMUs in use on the Southern region. The Class 387 is British-built by Bombardier and operated by Gatwick Express, and the Class 700 unit is German-built by Siemens at Krefeld and operated by Thameslink.

387208, 8 January 2016

387208 is seen having passed through Rugeley Trent Valley while on a mileage accumulation run to Crewe. The Class 387/2s had a troubled start to service due to safety considerations surrounding them being run as twelve-car driver-only operated units.

387212, 14 October 2017

387212 passes non-stop through Three Bridges while working south towards Brighton. The Class 387/2 units normally run in either eight-car formations or twelve-car formations during the peak hours.

387214, 10 May 2018

387214 is seen departing from Gatwick Airport while heading towards London Victoria with a non-stop Gatwick Express working. The Class 442 units that the Class 387 displaced ended up in storage for many months and are slowly coming back out and into service.

387216, 30 March 2016

387216 passes through Rugeley Trent Valley while on a mileage accumulation test run. The unit is seen carrying full Gatwick Express livery, complete with logos. This was running in a twelve-car formation along with classmates 387217 and 387218.

387221, 14 October 2017

387221 is seen running non-stop through Haywards Heath while heading towards London Victoria. In the distance some Southern-operated Class 377/3 units can be seen, stabled waiting for the afternoon peak service to commence.

387301, 17 October 2016

387301 passes through Rugeley Trent Valley while on a test run heading towards Wembley yard. There are just six Class 387/3s in service and all are in use with C2C, working out of London Fenchurch Street to Shoeburyness.

387303, 14 August 2017

387303 is seen passing through Barking with an empty stock move, heading towards London Fenchurch Street. The six Class 387/3s are used in two twelve-car formations, and are only used during the peak periods to increase capacity on the heavily used lines to Shoeburyness.

387305, 25 November 2016

387305 passes through Nuneaton, heading for Crewe on a test run. The Class 387/2 and Class 387/3 units were delivered before the Great Western Railway Class 387/1 units. The last unit off the Electrostar production line was 387174, eighteen years after the first unit, 357001, left Derby.